First of All I Wrote Your Name

Winston Plowes

Stairwell Books

Published by Stairwell Books
161 Lowther Street
York, YO31 7LZ

www.stairwellbooks.co.uk
@stairwellbooks

First of All I Wrote Your Name © 2025 Winston Plowes and Stairwell Books
Translations © Dr. Sher Ali (p15) and Gulnaz Kauser (pp17,19,28,34)

All rights reserved. No part of this publication may be reproduced, stored in or introduced into a retrieval system, or transmitted, in any form, or by any means (electronic, mechanical, photocopying, recording, e-book or otherwise) without the prior written permission of the author.

The moral rights of the author have been asserted.

ISBN: 978-1-939269-13-3
p18

Layout design: Alan Gillott
Decorative cutouts: Lisa Gort
Cover image: Tim Saunders

When I first learnt how to write,
first of all I wrote Your name.

> From 'The First Rain'
> by Nasir Kazmi
> (trans. Debjani Chatterjee)

For Basir

Acknowledgements

- Ghazal (To settle down Beside you) was first published online in The Ghazal Page, Winter Equinox Edition, December 2010.

- Ghazal (For you) was first published online in The Ghazal Page, September Equinox Edition, October 2011

- Ghazal (Could be Home) was first published in Mental Virus 8, 2010 and also in The Big Issue in The North Number 848 1-7 Nov 2010

- Ghazal (Pakistan) was first published in 'Love Islam' Poetry Anthology, Forward Press, Feb 2011

- Ghazal (Her Dad) / Ghazal (It Rained) / Ghazal (Beside You) / Ghazal (Could be Home) / Ghazal (Soft) all appeared in Chuneedha magazine, Bradford, September 2010

- Whalesong Ghazal (my song) was a commission for Leeds City Gallery, 2019.

- Ghazal (a journey) was published in Muse India, 2014

- Ghazal (Your letters) / Ghazal (Wrote in red) / Ghazal (It rained) were first published online in LYNX XXVII Feb 2012

- Wedding Ring was first published in Monkey Kettle #37 April 2012

Table of Contents

Traditional Ghazals 1
Ghazal #1 (after you) 3
Ghazal #2 (to settle down beside you) 4
Ghazal #3 (branches) 5
Ghazal #4 (time) 6
Ghazal #5 Reflections of a Dove 7
Ghazal #6 (a journey) 8
Ghazal #7 The Rain Still Falls in Pakistan 9
Ghazal #8 (deep) 10
Ghazal #9 (in snow) 11
Ghazal #10 (the day) 12
Ghazal #11 Whale Song Ghazal (my song) 13
Ghazal #11 Translation by Dr. Sher Ali 15
Ghazal #12 (but what now) 16
Ghazal #12 Translation by Gulnaz Kauser 17
Ghazal #13 (soft) 18
Ghazal #13 Translation by Gulnaz Kauser 19
Ghazal #14 (could be home) 20
Ghazal #15 (your hair) 21
Ghazal #16 (the eyes of a child) 22
Ghazal #17 (for you) 23
Ghazal #18 (her dad) 24
Ghazal #19 (it rained) 25
Ghazal #20 (just before dawn) 26
Ghazal #20 Translation by Gulnaz Kauser 28
Ghazal #21 (by it) 29
Ghazal #22 (your letters) 30
Ghazal #22 Translation by Gulnaz Kauser 31
Ghazal #23 (there) 32
Ghazal #24 (with the sun) 33
Ghazal #24 Translation by Gulnaz Kauser 34
Ghazal #25 (wrote in red) 35
Ghazal #26 (together) 36
Ghazal #27 (become a dragon) 37
Ghazal #28 (after the accident) 38

Free Verse Ghazals 39
100 Ways to Fold a Serviette 41
Wedding Ring 42
11 43
Porthleven 44
George Street Laundrette 45
Hymn 46
Safe House 47
Sheila's Wake 48
Meat Market 49
Time Stack 50
Lydia 51
Elmet 52
Park Life 53
Litmus 54
Woman in Black 55
Terminal 56
Appendices 57
Notes on the Ghazals 59
Further Reading 61
Index of Ghazals listed by refrain in alphabetical order 62
Some Notes on the Structure of an Urdu Ghazal 63
Criteria 64
Biographies 65

Traditional Ghazals

 *Ghazal #1*

An image remains after you
My heart has been tamed after you.

Whose is the name behind that smile?
Mystery is named after you.

If I could aim true I would draw
Cupid's arrow aimed after you.

With your eyes you guided my pen
Each sentence I framed after you.

As quickly as you came you went
My heart is left maimed after you.

Ghazal #2

I'd hide my blushing face to settle down beside you
And make a bed of lace to settle down beside you.

On a slab of watered marble polished over time
I trace a perfect place to settle down beside you.

Under a single star hidden by a lonely branch
The shadows cross my face to settle down beside you.

In a sea of racing winds and fraying homeless tides
I steal a seconds grace to settle down beside you.

Your single reward Winston, to guide you through the dark.
The only warm embrace to settle down beside you.

Ghazal #3

Solace: a bench beneath branches
Chi gathers underneath branches.

Dead man's fingers grope from the mire
Only tree on the heath branches.

A storm cannot pass through a sieve
Filing down the wind's teeth, branches.

For weeks the tree wore a white coat
Rime has frozen to sheath branches.

The names of all my lovers lost
Woven into a wreath's branches.

 **Ghazal #4**

(For Aleksander Samuel Bowden b.2010)

Earth making time
Man stretching time.

The gritstone's locked
It's hoarding time.

Seasons still rhyme
They're keeping time.

Life makes a mark
Birth's writing time.

Storms cover tracks
Erasing time.

Keep pace Winston
Stop marking time.

 **Ghazal #5 Reflections of a Dove**

(for Gaia)

Your searching face through the glass
Like the bird who knew the glass.

The feather that brushed your palm
Mirrored worlds that viewed the glass.

The blessings of earth and air
From both sides to you the glass.

Like two birds on cue, the glass
Love that's clear and true, the glass.

 ***Ghazal #6***

To heal the pain of loss, take a journey
And leave a trail of love, make a journey.

To hear Rumi for the very first time
And witness the whole earth quake – a journey!

To turn Ghalib's pages in many tongues
And try never to forsake a journey.

To read Shahid's last words and touch the light
But never disturb his wake – a journey.

To stand firm in the footsteps of giants
But be mindful not to fake a journey.

To follow, but not behind a blindfold
And advise when friends mistake a journey.

With one eye fixed on the future Winston
The other in the past – make a journey.

Ghazal #7
The Rain Still Falls in Pakistan

Your waters fill my mouth, my mother Pakistan
And yet I fear to swallow, sister Pakistan.

I'm holding my breath under the heaviest moons
Don't raise your fist in anger, brother Pakistan.

Many hands can cradle the path of the Indus
Rejoin my family, survivor Pakistan.

Names dissolved in your ripples, signatures erased
Rewriting history, another Pakistan.

 *Ghazal #8*

Through pure water deep
swam my daughter deep.

Her rhythmic breathing,
didn't falter, deep.

Broken reflections
memories alter – Deep.

Ghazal #9

My lungs heave, far from their best in snow.
Your cold words – froze in my chest, in snow.

Winter eggs are hatched for a struggle
The ice bird feathers its nest in snow.

Empty trees blown from Indian ink
Black and white snapshots at rest in snow.

Under the ice only mud and stones
Layers of time are compressed in snow.

Why did you leave me in this season?
Taunting promises that jest in snow.

Your guilty steps are heavy with lies
Yet I leave no trace, a test in snow.

Surrounded by ice just inches thick
Each white creaking step a quest in snow.

I planned to make this Christmas her best:
Winston – The unwelcome guest, in snow.

 *Ghazal #10*

Season slights of hand mistake the day.
Winter's hands churlishly take the day.

Filling the hours with witch hazel wine
Spring's hands slowly part, to make the day.

Kneading at time the clay oven cracks
Summer's hands lovingly bake the day.

Clutching corners of pressed cotton sheets
Autumn's hands violently shake the day.

Quartering time, love each season's turns
Poets tread softly to break the day.

Ghazal #11
Whale Song Ghazal (my song)

> We are the music-makers,
> And we are the dreamers of dreams,
> Wandering by lone sea-breakers...
> World losers and world forsakers,
> On whom the pale moon gleams:
> Yet we are the movers and shakers
> Of the world for ever, it seems.
>   – Arthur O'Shaughnessy

The Seven Seas mapping my song.

Hear the journey within my song.

My fin has cut the ocean's skin

Seabirds' calls mimicking my song.

Sing your name and I'll sing mine back

Clicks of time echoing my song.

Like a brush painting through water

Charcoal black skin tracing my song.

Slipping through a vast blue desert

Deep dark below weaving our song.

Call me blackfish call me sea ghost

Bubbles perforating my song.

In the cathedral of my bones

Shadows of lungs singing my song.

Deep shadows in shallow waters
The river strangling my song.

Stranded with my family pod
Gunshot and knife ending my song.

Ghazal #11
Translation by Dr. Sher Ali

نغمہٴ دل

ہم موسیقی کے خالق ہیں
ہم خوابوں کے نغمہ آرائی ہیں
تنہا لہروں کی طرح سرگرداں
تھے اک سے ہمارے اور ٹھہر جانے ہوئے
جن پر پیلا چاند منور ہے!
لیکن پھر بھی ہم ہی اصل محرک ہیں!
نغمہ ہیں جوش سے اگل پڑتا ہے...

Arthur O'Shaughnessy

سرک سی فرزدوں میں ہر لگتی کا نقش ہے
ہر لگتی میں اس فارک کو غور سے سنو

ہیں اپنے دست بازوس سے من دروں کا سننے چھوٹا ہوں
سنہری پرندے ہر لگتی کو فوق الفی سمجھتے ہیں

مجھے سہیلا چھلی او سمن دریب ہو تک کشتے ہیں!
جاب ہر سن غم کو شکست کرتے ہیں

پلیں سن اچکی تگاو اور ہیں پلی سن نظم کا لگی تگاوں گا!
وقت کی لوک منوں میں ہر لگتی تگ نچے ہیں!

ٹی کوس میبر شرکی طارد چویلن یپر مصوری کرتا ہو
چار کولہے بھی ہر لگتی کو یک منتقب ہیں ہے

وسی عمل گوری گنتیاں سن پیہلت ہے ہوئے
پت تک لڑی ہیں ہر لگتی تقیب ہے ہوئے

ہر یاست خوان کے یگر جگر ہیں
ہر یہ باطن ہیں چور گتی تک تصرو ک گی ہے!

کنگھر سین لیوں میں طول سنانے
دیا ہر لگتی کیا گل گ ہوٹ رہا ہے

ہمارے خلگی رشتوں سے نہلے ک!
بن دوق دار چا دوس سے ہر لگتی نلبو کی سے جا رہے ہیں

15

Ghazal #12

The anniversary, but what now?
I'm standing at your gate, but what now?

Will you shelter me, a stranger now
Or have I come too late, but what now?

Familiar sounds and scent of you
Can we forget the hate, but what now?

I have left a trail of fallen leaves
A rotting line of fate, but what now?

The years have been unfaithful to me
And I have travelled late, but what now?

Returning home to search for the past
And finding words that grate, but what now?

A lifetime travelling home Winston,
A struggle to relate, but what now?

Ghazal #12
Translation by Gulnaz Kauser

رفاقتوں کا حسیں زمانہ جو لوٹ آئے تو پھر بھی کیا ہے
مری صدا گر تمہارے در سے لپٹ ہی جائے تو پھر بھی کیا ہے
تو کیا تم اب بھی مجھ اسے گمنام اجنبی کو ساتھ دو گی
مگر نہ مہلت بھی لوٹ آئے کی بت جائے تو پھر بھی کیا ہے
ابھی فضاؤں میں ڈولنے ہے تمہاری خوشبو ، تمہارا لہجہ
ذرا جو کم ہوں نہ نعرتوں کے گھہرے سائے تو پھر بھی کیا ہے
جھپتے ، بے رنگ ، خسک بنوں کے ساتھ میں بھی بکھر رہا ہوں
حیراں نصیبی کے اس چمن میں بہار جھائے تو پھر بھی کیا ہے
گررہا جانا ہوں اسی بے نام زندگی سے قریب کھانا . سہم اٹھانا
جلے تو کیا ہے سمے کا چکر جو حل نہ پائے تو پھر بھی کیا ہے
گئے دنوں کی تلاش میں پھر سے اپنے گھر کو پلٹ پڑا ہوں
جدائی کی دلخراش ساعت جو سامہ آئے تو پھر بھی کیا ہے ..
کڑی مسافت میں وسعتیں میں گزار بیٹھا ہوں عمر ساری
سو اب وہ پہلی سی ٹھنڈی چھاؤں جو مل بھی جائے تو پھر بھی کیا ہے

 ***Ghazal #13***

Sea spray settles soft
Upon the land, soft.

Damp skin pimples spread
By autumn's hand, soft.

Barefoot steps linger
In the wet sand, soft.

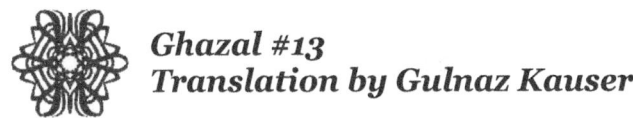

Ghazal #13
Translation by Gulnaz Kauser

بھیگی بھیگی موجیں گزریں دھیرے دھیرے
انجانے ساحل پہ اتریں دھیرے دھیرے
گیلے ہاتھ خزاں کے پھیلیں خشک فضا میں
سرد ہوائیں شجر کو جکڑیں دھیرے دھیرے
ننگے پائوں ریت پہ دور کو چلتے جائیں
نقش کسی رستے کے ابھریں دھیرے دھیرے

 ***Ghazal #14***

Your place could be home?
My place could be home?

For our love-locked hearts
Each place could be home.

For your land-locked clothes
My case could be home.

In our leg-locked race
This chase could be home.

For your lip-locked kiss
My face could be home.

Where I come to rest
That space could be home.

 ## Ghazal #15

Pearlescence of the moon, your hair.
The straight lines of a broom, your hair.

You held my hand, I kissed your eyes
And beauty filled the room, your hair.

I knew that it was meant to be
As brightness split the gloom, your hair.

The elven queens could weave your locks
Upon their golden looms, your hair.

It's strong enough to plait the rope
Which rang the bells of doom, your hair.

Your brushstrokes drew the final veil
The artist's hand that grooms your hair.

You wait for spring to come Winston
The primroses in bloom, your hair.

Ghazal #16

Look into the eyes of a child
Seeing through the eyes of a child.

A life as short as summer nights
Ever blue the eyes of a child.

The flash flood returned unannounced
Nothing new, the eyes of a child.

My memories ran through meadows
Never knew the eyes of a child.

She carries the grace inside her
Always through the eyes of a child.

Write your wishes in snow daddy
Dreams come true, the eyes of a child.

Ghazal #17

When you left me I died for you.
When you returned I cried for you.

We stumbled through each darkened room
I've always been a guide for you.

You dredged the depths of treachery
When you said no, I lied for you.

I ran the race just for your sake
With my last breath I sighed for you.

My love demanded more respect
In every way I tried for you.

When my heart cut off all those ties
The tears inside just dried for you.

 **Ghazal #18**

For Maisy

Dreaming of her dad
She's part of her dad.

Lost peg, heart-shaped hole
Her first love, her dad.

Her wish list complete
None above her dad.

You're all things Winston,
Hand and glove, her dad.

 *Ghazal #19*

The headlines read, "TODAY IT RAINED!"
Yet you just glibly say, "It rained".

You've watered down these yearning years
Ignoring each new day, it rained.

Green shoots of love were drowned at birth
You're flattening the hay - It rained.

The old tin roof's a xylophone!
But yet again you say, "It rained".

Without a coat you headed home
Whilst I count clouds of grey, it rained.

I want to soak up every drop
As others run away, it rained!

 *Ghazal #20*

It's the bluest hour just before dawn
And the coldest hour just before dawn.

Only true friends endure till daybreak
The loneliest hour just before dawn.

Tie down the tongue tethered in your head
The hungriest hour just before dawn.

That first kiss dangled there through the night
In the longest hour just before dawn.

If your heart survives you may be saved
It's the hardest hour just before dawn.

They wept in time to guttering flames
In the blackest hour just before dawn.

Sharpen your soul for the shadows war
In the bravest hour just before dawn.

Sirens moan and you can hear the sighs
In the noisiest hour just before dawn.

Look to the hills from where she'll return
In your lowest hour just before dawn.

Stroking the hair of a new born child
In the youngest hour just before dawn.

All your memories flew the attic
The emptiest hour just before dawn.

Pills wrapped in cling film, curtains still drawn
In the weakest hour just before dawn.

Why do you whisper old things my friend?
In the quietest hour just before dawn.

Ghazal #20
Translation by Gulnaz Kauser

 *Ghazal #21)*

The flood spared my cat, nuzzled by it.
Last remaining friend, snuggled by it.

The North Sea rolls, letters seldom come
Pen driven by doubt, riddled by it.

She said her kisses came from angels
But her faith was torn, muddled by it.

If the tide gets much higher he'll drown
Dog came home alone, troubled by it.

The pains came whenever he shouted
She's in the corner, doubled by it.

The dog watched cats, one ear up, one down
Its front leg quivered, trembled by it.

Her hair dyed blonde, her eyes painted black,
What colour's her heart? Puzzled by it.

The mouse made a nest in the spice drawer
Nutmeg, thyme and seeds nibbled by it.

Their god fell out of bed in the night
Tremors ran through them, rumbled by it.

Granddad worked down the mine all his life
I log on and type, humbled by it.

Ghazal #22

No love lost around your letters.
History tightly bound your letters.

Bitter fruit grows in barren soil
Buried underground, your letters.

Inside the drawer without the key
Prying fingers found your letters.

Thistle heads disguised as roses
Friendly words now frowned, your letters.

Dark words piled in a dark corner
A discarded mound, your letters.

Echoes rest in empty places
A faint distant sound, your letters.

Her ship will never dock Winston
Words have run aground – your letters.

Ghazal #22
Translation by GULNAZ KAUSER

مجھ تو رک سے حمار ہیں ہی تمہار سے نامے
گئے نو رک سے حصار ہیں ہی تمہار سے نامے
گلاب حفو رکی نو ک کلی نور سی چھ رہی ہے
چھایا ہوا زہر بہار ہیں ہی تمہار سے نامے
اِدھر گگ شوں ہیں اِدھی بستی ہی ہوئی ہیں
کسگرد موتے غار ہیں ہی تمہار سے نامے
یوں جھے لا لک بیپ ہول مر جھک سے سر ج کے کن
سو توب یاش کہزار ہیں ہی تمہار سے نامے
صدا سے توٹی ہوئی کو ہی لنگ شت جھے سے
اک اچی سے ہار ہیں ہی تمہار سے نامے
وہ یک ہوئے نجر زہن سے در پہوٹ رکلا
رہے دل سوگوار ہیں ہی تمہار سے نامے
نجات مشکل ہے ویٹ نہ پھو رسے ابتو
لر تکہ شتہ ک غبار ہیں ہی تمہار سے نامے

 **Ghazal #23**

For Kristján Unnar Kristjánsson

Northern lights plait cyan skies there.
Native auks still fear to fly there.

An empty shell pressed into sand
Where she left her last goodbyes there.

Searching through the jumbled houses
And finding seabirds lost cries there.

We are shingle as the tide turns
Waiting for the waves, we lie there.

The beacons burned where love first struck
It's dark now – so why am I there?

 *Ghazal #24*

The canal's life, like exposed film, living with the sun.
Slick oiled fish rising to vanish, sinking with the sun.

A ribbon of life threaded between retaining hills
Settling into the green cleft, shrinking with the sun.

The wakes of golden goslings ruffling through the reeds.
Newborn ferns bowing their coiled heads thinking with the sun.

A million wings go about their tiny business
The windswept miracles of life drinking in the sun.

My life is stronger now it is woven with the water
The rhythm of life, unchained days linking with the sun.

Ghazal #24
Translation by Gulnaz Kauser

لگتا ہے پھر پر اک جہاں سورج کے سنگ
ٹوٹتی ہے اک مچھلی ابھی ہاں سورج کے سنگ
چوٹی پر بیٹھا تھا جو نیس تکا مو مو ہمل
ٹوٹا جدا مرے وادی ہر کہاں سورج کے سنگ
بلگتی مرغی ورکا شور گلی یگ ہاں سر پر
پیلی ارک چھرو چھی مریب ے اماں سورج کے سنگ
کہولے مریر رہنے دنک ے حسین آغاز پر
چلن لگتا امیں دور کا جہاں سورج کے سنگ
زندگی ک ھری ہے مری پھر ورک ے بطس ے
بتا جدا ہوں ہں مجھ سب کے راس سورج کے سنگ

 *Ghazal #25*

Despite his temper, he never wrote in red.
He would have lost if he ever wrote in red.

His suicide note spoke of both lust and death
"All my lights went out", his lover wrote in red.

After the knife blade, their palms smudged the future
"Till death do us part", blood brothers wrote in red.

Your mother's case notes speak clearly of madness
Barely legible, the doctor wrote in red.

"Winston will never amount to anything"
My final report – The teacher wrote in red.

 **Ghazal #26**

We live apart each day together
But in our hearts we stay together.

In a theatre of dreams we sing
Our songs dance a ballet together.

Distances between leave room to grow
We'll never overstay together.

The camera's eye cannot shed tears
Pictures of love portrayed together.

Constant reunion lights the fires
Like smoke and flames we play together.

Life is brief yet love everlasting
Our chosen vows we say together.

Of all the stars you have searched Winston
We share this Milky Way together.

 ## Ghazal #27

"The ancient sages said, do not despise the snake for having no horns, for who is to say it will not become a dragon? So may one just man become an army".
  –   The Water Margin, BBC TV (dubbed version). 1976

Could we in our own way, become a dragon?
Could love to my dismay, become a dragon?

Poison one soft word in a child's lullaby.
And each little lamb may become a dragon.

Do not despise the snake for having no horns.
For he too, may one day become a dragon.

Each man's wish is a single spark from the grate.
Fed spirits and tales, they become a dragon.

He died in his sleep, a spade found beside him.
Did the squaddie at play become a dragon?

Page ten: A quick spell to banish Prince Charming.
Count to seven and say, "Become a dragon".

Veneered brains queued deep well after hours, "Winston"
"It's your round" they slurred, "Stay, Become a dragon".

 *Ghazal #28*

Innocence supposed after the accident
New facts were disclosed after the accident.

Flowers wrapped in paper, letters wrapped in guilt
With no cheques enclosed after the accident.

His life contracted to a six-foot circle
In his chair he dozed after the accident.

They left their dreams in a mangled bush shelter
The door never closed after the accident.

He scooped with his hands when the spoon let him down
That's when she proposed after the accident.

Yours was the last hand to sign the book Winston
Mourners stood composed after the accident.

Free Verse
Ghazals

 ## *100 Ways to Fold a Serviette*

A single candle
On your birthday.

We will never debate
The apostrophe.

The padlocked playground
Where poplars still cried.

There are backspaces
In my world ever since.

He'll never recover
But may learn to cope.

A gravestone lost
To untended grass.

There were reasons
She left no note as such.

The killing words lie
In the creases of life:

"Sorry... I dont
Love you anymore".

There are a hundred ways
To fold a serviette.

 **Wedding Ring**

For Sarah

I wonder where you run to
Your face hidden behind hands.

Your nightmares are spiral bound
Flat and under his radar.

Moonlight fell on the god-house
Looks peaceful from the outside.

Where the raining never stops
And all your clothes are dirty.

The fire escape seems likely
To be a place for blood stains.

Counting bruises in her head
All of them under the skin.

His temper smouldered for years
With no air getting to it.

Reflection in the window
Is it you or is it me.

11

Three Minutes silence
Fills an afternoon.

Pack the son away
In too safe a place.

In your hour of need
Clocks ticked too quickly.

The soundman struggles
To maintain levels.

A police siren
Serenades the lost.

 ***Porthleven***

I've travelled to you all day
But my heart remains at home.

The sun soaks the fields to life
As winter thumbs its pages.

Darkness lived beneath his eyes
The shadows under the bridge.

The larch needles yellowing
Some one has to be different.

Your message vibrates my phone
And I shudder as it lights.

Leaves race across the mud flats
Distracting the herons aim.

She yawned away her summer
Putting cherries in her cheeks.

George Street Laundrette

It was raining on the inside
The school playground, long since emptied.

The bus swung out to avoid him
Bullying the oncoming cars.

He didn't bend in the middle
His wife watched his head hit the road.

Over the wall, the canal froze
And I could find no trace of them.

My sock always folded in pairs
By hands that needed so much more.

 ***Hymn***

Hair fell at her feet
Cushioning her prayers.

Her silhouette set
Against changing winds.

The cold nights drove in
Hid between her ribs.

Pew seats polished hard
Lessons harder still.

Dust cannot settle
On a turning page.

 ## Safe House

The glass fell on the carpet
Haemorrhaging Côtes du Rhône.

In an old exercise book
I scribbled my life story.

Our girls had grown out of him
Abandoned both their parents.

As a last resort he knew
His wife couldn't run in heels.

I saw more through one good eye
Than he ever did through two.

 ## Sheila's Wake

Unfathomable birds
Panning gold with their wings.

Pugilists of the road
Punch drunk into the wind.

Too many black skins flit
Through this mild December.

Look back into red eyes
Too far back for a spring.

Like a spreading disease
Light starts to fail at three.

They must eat to get home
Their stomachs full of lies.

 ***Meat Market***

The queue never ends at the meat stall
Where spendthrift mothers jostle for fat.

His shirt clashed with the upholstery
Always sat with the light behind him.

They cheat at the self-scan checkout till
Potatoes are cheaper than kiwis.

I Love Wigan it said on her top
Her cracked lips said something different.

Have you heard, if you swallow a pin
It works its way out through your finger?

# Time Stack

You live a little
You die a little.

On the Bersham Tip
I could see his dot.

Sliding like Sunday
down the rills of spoil.

Same all the way through
Like your simple life.

The motorway hums
less in the evening.

Flowers fight through cracks
This is not my Wales.

 ## *Lydia*

Fixed like a knot in wood
Polished by her shuffles.

She undressed next to me
Silks gave way to goose bumps.

 ***Elmet***

Their bed was a ploughshare
For burying false dreams.

Clinging to the hillside
By sentences cut short.

Winds that toppled gravestones
Erased inscriptions first.

Posthumous birthday cards
Stood on the mantelpiece.

Fishing for reflections
In a pool of ripples.

 ***Park Life***

Shadows live up old trees
Folded into their bark.

You could tell by his smile
The lad carried a gun.

Page twenty three came first
She had burnt out the rest.

They wound down their windows
to check that life was real.

Gravity pulls stronger
The heavier your heart.

 **Litmus**

She walks home whilst reading books
Autumn turning the pages.

A head, stuffed full of murders
it's bleeding between the lines.

The auburn hair and square jaw
had skipped two generations.

Blue shoes leave shallow footprints
Cracked soles sucking up puddles.

Joining up the dots of life
but never making pictures.

Blossom blocks up the gutters
And it's all but over now.

 ## Woman in Black

Candles lose their summer scent
Hijacked by this November.

The studded door slowly slammed
And darkness painted her face.

Wax under the fingernails
The only clue required.

Bees set into a black mass
Staining all that they covered.

Crows on the mausoleum
Lied when they said they would stay.

 **Terminal**

Too many dreams of leaving
left a shadow in her bed.

This house was never a home
It's time to draw the curtains.

She Became as pale as soap
Robbed of the scent of roses.

Partly taken medicines
filled the bedside cabinet.

The girl with the ginger hair
befriended the flightless crane.

Stains grew up the weary walls
The clock ticked incessantly.

Appendices

Notes on the Ghazals

Ghazal #3 (branches) – Matla taken from *Ghazal 12, Bones in Their Wings: A Series of Ghazals*, Lorna Crozier, Hagios Press. 2003.

Ghazal #6 (a journey) – Jalāl ad-Dīn Muḥammad Rūmī (1207-1273). Mirza Asadullah Baig Khan (Ghalib) (1797-1869). Agha Shahid Ali (1949-2001).

Ghazal #11 Whale Song Ghazal – Was a commission for Leeds City Museum in 2019. The poem is on permanent display together with the skeleton of the Long-finned Pilot Whale in the entrance to the downstairs gallery.

Ghazal #14 (could be home) – Awarded 2nd Prize in The Big Scribble poetry competition, 2010 and published in The Big Issue Magazine.

Ghazal #20 – *"When my son was an infant in Paris, we woke together in the light the French call l'heure bleue, between darkness and day, between the night of a soul and its redemption, an hour associated with pure hovering."* Carolyn Forché, Blue Hour, Bloodaxe Books. 2003.

Ghazal #23 (there) – Inspired by the landscape photography of Kristján Unnar Kristjánsson.
http://photographyblogger.net/gorgeous-icelandic-landscapes-by-kristjan-unnar-kristjansson/

Ghazal #26 (together) – Line five adapted from the lyrics by Canadian prog' rock band Rush, "The spaces in between / Leave room / For you and I to grow". *Permanent Waves.* (1980).

Time Stack – The Bersham Tip is a large spoil heap of colliery slag near Wrexham, Wales. Controversially, It has been earmarked for flattening.

Elmet – Was an independent kingdom of in the 5th and 6th century and later refers to a smaller region approximating to the West Riding of Yorkshire.

Further Reading

Generations of Ghazals: Ghazals by Nasir Kazmi and Basir Sultan Kazmi, ed. Debjani Chatterjee, Redbeck Press, 2003

The Night Abraham Called to the Stars, Robert Bly, Harper Collins, 2001

Call Me Ishmael Tonight, Agha Shahid Ali, W.W.Norton & Co, 2003

The Clerk's Tale, Spencer Reece, Houghton Mifflin Books, 2004

Jim Harrison, Outlyer and Ghazals, Simon and Schuster, 1969

Bones in their Wings: Ghazals, Lorna Crozier, Hagios Press, 2003

The Enlightened Heart (An Anthology of sacred Poetry) Edited by Stephen Mitchell Harper & Row 1989

Masterpieces of Urdu Ghazal K.C. Kanda, Sterling Paperbacks 1992

Ravishing Disunities: real Ghazals in English, Agha Shahid Ali, Weslyan Poetry series, 2000

The Fact of a Doorframe, Adrianne Rich, WW Norton & Co, 1994

Index of Ghazals listed by refrain in alphabetical order –

a journey, **8**
after the accident, **38**
after you, **3**
become a dragon, **37**
branches, **5**
but what now, **16**
by it, **29**
could be home, **20**
deep, **10**
for you, **23**
her dad, **24**
in snow, **11**
it rained, **25**
just before dawn, **26**, **28**
soft, **18**, **19**
the day, **12**
the eyes of a child, **22**
the glass, **7**
there, **32**
time, **6**
to settle down beside you, **4**
together, **36**
whale song, **13**, **15**
with the sun, **33**, **34**
wrote in red, **35**
your hair, **21**
your letters, **30**, **31**

Some Notes on the Structure of an Urdu Ghazal

A Template

```
-------------------------- A (x)
-------------------------- B (x)

---------------------------------
-------------------------- C (x)

---------------------------------
-------------------------- D (x)

---------------------------------
-------------------------- E (x)

--------------(y)---------------
-------------------------- F (x)
```

Example

Ghazal

Season slights of hand forsake the day
Winter's hands stealthily take the day

Filling the light with witch hazel wine
Spring's hands slowly part, to make the day

Kneading at time the clay oven cracks
Summer's hands lovingly bake the day

Clutching corners of pressed cotton sheets
Autumn's hands violently shake the day

Quartering time, love seasons in turn
Move gently Winston to wake the day

Criteria

1) The title of the poem is 'Ghazal'.
2) There are five or more couplets (Shers).
3) The second line of each couplet ends with the same word (or string of words). This is the Refrain (Radif) '(x)'. 'the day' in the example.
4) Each Radif is directly preceded by the Rhyme (Qafia) 'A-F'. Forsake, take, make, bake etc in the example.
5) The first sher (Matla) is special and has Radif and Qafia in both of its lines.
6) The last sher (Maqta) is also special and contains the poet's signature (Takkhalus) (y). 'Winston' in the example. This can be an actual name, part of a name or a pen name and can appear anywhere in the Maqta.
7) The meter (Behr) of the poem is consistent. Every line should have the same number of syllables. Nine in the example.
8) Each sher should be a poem in itself. There is no enjambment between the lines of each sher or direct connection between shers.
9) Traditionally the subject of the whole poem is love and loss.

This is only a basic description of the criteria. There are many ghazals that do not exhibit all nine criteria and there are also different types of ghazal and variations within them. Personally, I feel that these criteria are only important if they are important to you and you are trying to create a traditional Urdu ghazal in English. Which incidentally is no easy matter and perhaps a contradiction in itself.

Biographies

Winston Plowes

Winston Plowes teaches creative writing and art in schools and works with adult groups across Calderdale and beyond. His last joint collection, *Tales from the Tachograph*, was published jointly with Gaia Holmes in 2018 by Calder Valley Poetry. He is based aboard his floating home near Hebden Bridge where he receives regular advice from his friends and spiritual advisers, the Canada geese he calls Ringo and Maureen.

Timsperstectiveart

For twenty years I have used Perspective as a means to explore reality, and to search for new understandings within subjects, each reality experienced by the viewer is unique and changes with continued study. The cover art for this book was inspired by traditional geometric Persian art and reflects the depths and complexities of competing forces within the written word and within ourselves as humans.

Sher Ali

Dr. Sher Ali holds a PhD in the tradition of Urdu poetry in England from Punjab University, Lahore. In his research, he highlighted the vital role of Mr. Plowes, who has written Urdu Ghazals in English by following the traditional meter and poetic background. Important work promoting harmony between English and Urdu poetry.

Gulnaz Kauser

Gulnaz Kausar is a respected and contemporary voice in modern Urdu poetry, well-versed in both the spirit and structure of the language. Born in Lahore, Pakistan, she studied Law before completing her Master's in Urdu and English Literature. She worked at the Research and Publication Department of the National College of Arts (NCA) and later the Government College University. Her debut collection, *Khawab Ki Hathili Par (On the Palm of a Dream)* was published in 2012 and her second collection, *Maya* has gained recent critical acclaim.

Ghazal [Could be home] *by Winston Plowes is an inspiring attempt at a difficult classical Persian form. The result is spare, direct and forceful, capturing the complex in simple language.*

Judging Panel, The Big Scribble

You handle the traditional form of the ghazal very well.

Lorna Crozier

An English poet has successfully managed to write ghazals that, on the one hand, fulfil all the technical conditions required by the genre, and on the other, have a new flavour, hitherto unknown to the form.

I think you have come as close to the ghazal form as is possible in English.

Basir Sultan Kazmi

When I listen to Winston reading his ghazals in English I hear them in Urdu.

Nabia Jameel

Stylish, deft and heartfelt writing that shows us form can mean freedom

Helen Mort

Other anthologies and collections available from Stairwell Books

Sleeve Heart	Eleanor May Blackburn
Goldfish	Jonathan Aylett
Strike	Sarah Wimbush
Marginalia	Doreen Hinchliffe
The Estuary and the Sea	Jennifer Keevill
In | Between	Angela Arnold
Quiet Flows the Hull	Clint Wastling
Lunch on a Green Ledge	Stella Davis
there is an england	Harry Gallagher
Iconic Tattoo	Richard Harries
Herdsmenization	Ngozi Olivia Osuoha
On the Other Side of the Beach, Light	Daniel Skyle
Words from a Distance	Ed. Amina Alyal, Judi Sissons
Fractured	Shannon O'Neill
Unknown	Anna Rose James, Elizabeth Chadwick Pywell
When We Wake We Think We're Whalers from Eden	Bob Beagrie
Awakening	Richard Harries
Starspin	Graehame Barrasford Young
A Stray Dog, Following	Greg Quiery
Blue Saxophone	Rosemary Palmeira
Steel Tipped Snowflakes 1	Izzy Rhiannon Jones, Becca Miles, Laura Voivodeship
Where the Hares Are	John Gilham
The Glass King	Gary Allen
Gooseberries	Val Horner
Poetry for the Newly Single 40 Something	Maria Stephenson
Northern Lights	Harry Gallagher
More Exhibitionism	Ed. Glen Taylor
Lodestone	Hannah Stone
Learning to Breathe	John Gilham
Throwing Mother in the Skip	William Thirsk-Gaskill
New Crops from Old Fields	Ed. Oz Hardwick
The Ordinariness of Parrots	Amina Alyal

For further information please contact rose@stairwellbooks.com

www.stairwellbooks.co.uk
@stairwellbooks

www.ingramcontent.com/pod-product-compliance
Lightning Source LLC
LaVergne TN
LVHW091319080426
835510LV00007B/554